AF355615

Broken Psalms

Alexis A. Holmes

Copyright © Alexis A. Holmes
All Rights Reserved.

This book has been self-published with all reasonable efforts taken to make the material error-free by the author. No part of this book shall be used, reproduced in any manner whatsoever without written permission from the author, except in the case of brief quotations embodied in critical articles and reviews.

The Author of this book is solely responsible and liable for its content including but not limited to the views, representations, descriptions, statements, information, opinions, and references ["Content"]. The Content of this book shall not constitute or be construed or deemed to reflect the opinion or expression of the Publisher or Editor. Neither the Publisher nor Editor endorse or approve the Content of this book or guarantee the reliability, accuracy, or completeness of the Content published herein and do not make any representations or warranties of any kind, express or implied, including but not limited to the implied warranties of merchantability, fitness for a particular purpose.

The Publisher and Editor shall not be liable whatsoever...

Made with ❤ on the BookLeaf Publishing Platform
www.bookleafpub.in
www.bookleafpub.com

Dedication

For the would be weary, but willing to pour & hold on a little longer.

Preface

Being a believer doesn't suddenly answer all of life's questions. However, somewhere between wrestling with God, ourselves, and the word there is resolve and peace that surpasses even our own understanding. This collection of pieces is a brief insight on the mind of just one believer. May something written minister to you.

Acknowledgements

1 Corinthians 1:27

Made a fool of
Doing donuts of disappointments,
& spinning out into cynicism
Nothing groundbreaking to account for,
Yet keeping a trace of a testimony on the tongue
Made low with the whispers of elevation,
but the valleys are all too familiar-
& lilies few and far between

Robbed of the joy of dreams,
But suddenly given new ones
Rug pulled from beneath me,
Yet told to stand firm

I had fainted lest I believed

Matthew 7:7

Questions aren't insulting to a God who tells us
to ask, seek, and knock.
Isn't it the glory of God to conceal a thing
and the glory of man to uncover it?
 Aren't his mysteries are revealed to those in proximity?
 Did you want a middleman?

 Did you truly want an answer,
Or simply a way out of the process?

There are things others can't answers
And answers you won't accept from others
It is no crime, no sin to ask
But have you first questioned the motives of your heart?

Do you ask selfishly?
Do you ask in contention?
Do you ask for clarity?
Do you ask in greed?

 Do you ask in vengeance?
 Do you ask in righteousness?
Do you ask from a pace of repentance AND forgiveness?

Do you ask willing to yield to even an undesirable answer?

Do you ask in humility acknowledging the confine of the human mind?

 Would you be willing to be still for a thorough response?

 Would you sift your answer through the word?

How long would you study to find solution, to read and read again?

How many times do you ask before walking away?

 Have you learned to abide even in the quiet?

 Do you ask truly believing you'd get a response?

 Would you ask again?

Colossians 3:23

If you cook, feed someone
 If you create, put something into perspective
 If you compose, make souls dance
 If you're good with numbers, count the costs
 If you care, look after those who need it
 If you're sensitive, soften hearts
 If you're intense, lead the transformation
 If you've got a Colgate smile, brighten the world
 If you ooze intensity, draw out authenticity
If you exist, reflect what brought you into existence

Ecclesiastes 3:11

I hand hung every star
 that takes your breath away
 I drew the lines of the waves
 that move you from thousands of miles away
 I fluffed every cloud you gaze at for hours
Show me my error
 Tell me where I made a mistake on you,
 My handmade Claymation

I angled your eyes for a specific point of view
 & If I so chose to remove your sight
 Remember I'm always protecting your vision
I gave you ears to hear
 & If I so chose to shut them
 I keep you in a comfortable silence
I parted your lips enough
 For my words to escape & my tone to be translated
 Project what I placed in you

I took my time with you
 I poured my life, my breath, my Spirit in you
 Do you think you can design a vessel to carry that
weight?

I made you one of a kind
& Even if I manufactured similar editions
 A trained eye always knows the difference
I didn't mold you to be held by all
I didn't tune you to play for every composition
I don't create my jigsaw pieces to fit every corner
 I have a place for you
 I made you like me

And I make everything beautiful in its time.

Exodus 33:18

You want to know what I look like? Why?
 To attach yourself to my deity based off appearances?
 Many have an appearance of my righteousness but,
 lack the power thereof

 It's hard to not look like me,
 when I made humanity in my image
Whether you look like the nations of old,
 a common face or a foreigner in passing,
 If you follow me, you're mine.

Who can't I save? Who won't I save?
 Is my grace is only sufficient for certain skin shades?
 Skin can't save you from where your spirit take you
 What is the substance of your faith without a color base

 Seek my face for features culture can't capture

Genesis 16:13

He sees the smoke, the spark, the flame
 He sees the yield
He sees the redemption arc
 He sees the byproduct of his handy work
He sees success.
He sees joy
He sees his seal
He sees remnant
He sees soil stirred for planting
He sees the truth
He sees his breath not wasted
He sees anticipation of his glory
& humanity's marvel of his miracles

He sees a beauty only he can detect,
enabling others to see the same
He sees durability
He sees one who also sleeps through the storms
He sees changes of a pure heart
He sees preparedness
He sees momentum
He sees willingness
He sees attempts to bridle the tongue
He sees his design

He sees his word never returning void

He sees his fruit

He sees faithfulness

He sees arms stretched out

He sees living sacrifice

 He sees worthy election

He sees provision

He sees a finished work,

a finished thing from it beginning

He sees resolve

He sees you

Genesis 8:21

Does it linger
Is it short lived
Is it detectable
Is it memorable
Is it good

How long does it last?
Would you share what it is?
Can it been washed away?
Is it strong enough to taste?

Does it ease the sinuses,
or burn the eyes
Is it brought out for everyday use,
or only special occasions, for show or looksies
Are people drawn towards you,
or scattered from your presence

Every scent isn't for everyone.
But those who desire will inquire
So trail them to the Lord

James 4:8

When God asks where's my hug:
 I count the steps between us
 & realize my shoes aren't worthy to reach out to his
arms
 As If I could get there on my own in my own strength
He paves a path of gentleness and warmth
 No shoes, bare soles- its holy ground

When God asks where's my hug:
 I sand off to the side never out of site
 Trying to gauge the width of his arms
The span of his muscles
The height of his wings
My eyes don't see far enough in the distance

When God asks where's my hug,
 & When I'm coming home:
I don't cringe, I don't shy away in fear

Yet I am frozen.

Like I have the fragments of an heirloom behind my
back
 & to hug me is to see my scarred hands & guilty eyes

I know he already knows.
I don't deserve a hug.
But I also know that he's known to offer grace
underserved
 & I shouldn't be afraid or stuck or distant
 But I can't pry my feet to move closer

Too feeble to knock
 the door isn't locked, his back isn't turned.
 He hasn't forsaken nor forgotten,
 So why won't I move my feet toward him?
I'll stand here & recall the warmth of his last hug
 So maybe his memory would move me

When God ask where's his hug
 I'll say right here
 My heart still beats for you

Jeremiah 29:11

I'm not dangling my glory to tease
I want your desire & your capacity
to hold what is in store

My intent is to walk you
beyond the element of surprise,
into knowing expectation.
Hope fulfilled.
I'll reveal:
what you would've settled for in the past
& the greatness you've yet to behold

I intend to develop endurance for the race
Appreciation for the practice runs
Craving for victory
Humility in showing up, being present
& Good sportsmanship

I intend to display my distinct signature
I mean to show my fingerprint in your mold
I purpose you with sharpness & strategy to pierce
through darkness
showcasing the swordsmanship of my army-
armed with my word

I designed you yielding to boundaries,
 tethered to my heavenly ordinances

 I orchestrated the instrument of your mind, mouth, &
movement
 down to the small gestures you don't quite catch
 I planned every cut, dye, braid and twist
 of every follicle of every strand of hair on your head

 I did it on purpose
 To prosper you in my ways
 To protect you in my arms
 To teach you my truth, the only truth
 To guide your yoke in a land of milk & honey
 & vegetation you've yet to dream of

I purposed you with limits
 to reveal what it means to serve a God with none

I meant it when I made you
 As I made you,
 Where I placed you
 Simply let me reshape you

 Let me take you through my preplanned ventures
 I've yet to reveal so you don't wander aimlessly
 I know what I'm doing

I've done it for centuries predating even time itself

Its on purpose you know

John 12:24

Just in case things get worse
Just know it can and might grow darker
Do not be shaken or quenched out of hope
Keep your heart soft,
And eyes to the lilies in the valley
Day will break

Joshua 24:23

Don't you dare say you're following me
 When you're meandering in the opposite direction
 You're distorting how the sheep hear my voice
 You got some nerve speaking my name with your
deception
You confuse my face with my creation
 But you wouldn't be the first generation
You think you could name my power
 Confine its fullness in your hands?

I'll consume this earth in seconds
 & make the sediment of the solar system dance
Do you think you can summon me
 With dirty dances & unrepentant cries
 Why do you think we're on good terms
 When you've perverted the truth I left behind

You sit emptying your mind
 Receiving whoever & whatever drops in
 Don't mistake that for me-
 I only come through personal invitation
 Intentional reservation
 A choice of surrendered belief

You must not *know* me well
Maybe I'm so big you missed me
Or so deep in the details you strain to see
But I know you've encountered my children
My word is buried in the bowels of my beloved vessels,
with MY Spirit I filled & planted them
I prune the yielded seed
You can't praise me in ways that don't please me
I'm repulsed by strange smoke
I just dropped in to clear the air

Acts 5:42

The pews aren't quite dusty
So I know you've been by recently
The lights are dim
But the glow is still seen for miles

There aren't many members
But the visitors of value frequent

There is something to be said
Something to be read
Something to be shared
Even the crumbs or leftovers
will feed my sheep

The pool of living waters still flows
A stream, a drip, a leak
Soon enough someone will be by to stir
Clean the windows, Empty the closets
Consecrate room for the king

This is more hallow than hollow,
a dwelling place for tears
A shielding warmth, a safe-haven
A refinery, a training ground

A well of wisdom-
If only you'd dig deeper

Matthew 6:13

When temptation knocks,
 Deadbolt the door

 It will seep in wherever it can,
 So guard your gates
A seductive suggestion
 May start as a joke, a thought or
 Something innocently stumbled upon
 Don't give it a foothold
It will prowl, seeking to devour,
 Run.
 There is distinction between fear and caution

 But if you are caught in its claws, its teeth
 and you succumb to appetite-
 Yours or its,
 Turn back to the way for renewal
 & do something different next time

Matthew 6:21

First give your heart,
 & your mind will follow
Give your mind,
 & your feet will follow

Give your steps,
 & your hands will follow
Give the work of your hands
 & your habits will follow

Give your habits,
 & your lifestyle will follow
Give your lifestyle,
 your career & dreams will follow

Give your career & your dreams,
 & your treasure will follow
Give your treasure,
 Your heart will follow

Psalm 46:10

I do more in a blink
than you do in a full lifetime
You're caught off by the time,
I hold the stopwatch
Put some life in your voice
Speak like your words hold weight
Be still and know, or at least try to remember

Proverbs 16:19

We're not building from scratch.
 There is no charge to create a new blueprint,
 but to learn, explore, & operate in the one already
drawn.
We are building from a reflection of infinite glory,
 that has chosen us for a time such as this.
 Plan on it, plan for it,
 And if it falls through, do it again.

Psalm 34:8

A new thing, who could know it?
If we knew it, timed it, guessed it, gauged it-
it wouldn't be new would it?

I trust you.
There shouldn't be a but,
after I say I trust you-
But there is.

Would you offer a crumb of revelation?
A pinch of a preview of an expected end?
Perhaps I could lick the mixing bowl of your mysteries,
& imagine what is to be.

But, no one gets a slice of unbaked cake
So we wait for your timing.
I trust your recipe,
I will taste & see

Psalm 39:3-4

Remember the ignite,
 You were full of life
 & hard for four walls to contain
 A candle lit was not meant to be hidden
 Even, in the process of being sustained
Life may smother the excitement
 But the final gasps of faith reign true
 When the zeal of combustion died down,
 Did you think HIS promises did too?

The flicker you can't see,
 is yet shut up in your bones
 Embers of endurance-
 What site to behold
 A weapon of mass destruction,
 Meant to make ashes of strongholds
The flame that scorches also refines
 The light that brings comfort, yet also blinds
 Live in warmth & wisdom to wield the power inside

Let the wind of the word
 Clear the haze
 Where there's smoke there is fire
 The lamps at your feet

will lead you in the way
So, walk while weeping
Don't you know your tears are jarred
Through the mire of the valleys
He still sees who you are-
A spark of his promises,
Fulfilled thus far

Bring enough oil for the journey,
Trim the burnt ends as you go
The darker it gets out here,
the brighter you glow
Look around,
It gets hard to spot the difference
But in faith play a game of I spy
& see that even I AM is in this Burn still
Burn Slow, Burn Bright, Burn Still.

Psalm 5:8

God, I'm not questioning you
 but, I have Questions

Where are we going?
Are we there yet?
How much longer will it take?
How many more plot holes- I mean potholes will we hit?
We already passed the rest stop for this leg, haven't we?
Can I guess what's around the way?
I'd likely underestimate the size of it.
Have you been taking off guards this whole time?
Limited vision, minimal sight, on and off numbness yet
you still request me?
What part of your glory is this for?
Aren't there other ways to prove your point?

You really want me to place all my bets on you?
What am I supposed to tell them?
How long do silence, shoulder shrugs, & vague plans
work?
Why do you have me here?
What am I supposed to be doing?
Why should I ask when you already know?

You know what...
Can we just stop by swings,
Pick up some sweet tea
& watch you transition the landscape
Count sheep and watch cows
That seems simpler than this- whatever this is

Why'd you give me a map,
 that only makes sense when you translate it
Why do you speak when I dream
 but seem silent when I wake
What are we doing
 It won't always be like this right?

Romans 8:28

Do you truly love the Lord?
Did you notice ALL things?
Not only good things, or some things
All things.

Unspeakable things
 that were never in the perfect will
Uncomfortable things
 that break you out or break you
Unpredictable things that shake up everything
Ugly things
 that seem better concealed but never stay away long
enough

Beautiful things
 that are less permanent than eternity
Things that made you a public spectacle,
 or awkward dinner debate
Things only seen in the secret place

So yes, even this.

2 Peter 1:10

Why not you?

Why not me?
 Is that supposed to be a trick question?

No. Why not you?
What do you think I can't reform?
Don't you know I made enough of you for you?
I know your faults & flaws but,
I still want you.
What can't I cleanse you of?
What can't I work for your good & my glory?
Have you underestimated my abilities,
or arc you testing how much you trust you?

You're not late,
I've been curating you.
You are not unworthy,
I appraise worth.

I didn't hold you back to insult you,
I taught you patience.

I exposed your insufficiencies to reveal my sufficiency-

I taught you humility.
 I didn't mar you,
 I marked you for a keen eye.
Why not you?
I chose you, I call for you.
My sheep, my child,
My jewel, my design,
My image, my creation
My name bearer, my vessel
Why. Not. You?

www.ingramcontent.com/pod-product-compliance
Lightning Source LLC
LaVergne TN
LVHW010926200726

843509LV00013B/2099